DISCOVERING
THE SONGHAY EMPIRE

LAURA LA BELLA

ROSEN
PUBLISHING®

New York

Published in 2014 by The Rosen Publishing Group, Inc.
29 East 21st Street, New York, NY 10010

Library of Congress Cataloging-in-Publication Data

La Bella, Laura, author.
Discovering the Songhay Empire/Laura La Bella.—First edition.
    pages cm—(Exploring African civilizations)
Includes bibliographical references and index.
ISBN 978-1-4777-1885-8 (library binding)
1. Songhai Empire—Juvenile literature. 2. Songhai (African people)—History—
Juvenile literature. 3. Africa, West—History—To 1884—Juvenile literature. I. Title. II.
Series: Exploring African civilizations.
DT532.27.L32 2014
966.2018—dc23

2013026240

Manufactured in the United States of America

CPSIA Compliance Information: Batch #W14YA: For further information, contact Rosen Publishing, New York, New York, at 1-800-237-9932.

A portion of the material in this book has been derived from *The Songhay Empire* by David Conrad.

CONTENTS

INTRODUCTION

The Songhay Empire occupied a region located in western Africa. From Gao, the empire's centrally located capital city on the Niger River, the Songhay held territory that expanded in all directions: from the Atlantic Ocean on the west to what is now northwest Nigeria and western Niger. From the early fifteenth to the late sixteenth century,

A man pulls a fishing net along the Niger River, the main waterway that flows through what used to be the Songhay Empire. The empire had numerous settlements along the banks of the river.

Songhay was one of the largest Islamic empires in history. It was also one of the last of three great empires that existed in the Western Sudan, a vast geographical region south of the Sahara Desert and north of the forest belt of coastal West Africa. The empire developed along both sides of the Niger River, a 2,600-mile (4,184-kilometer) waterway that flowed in a great curve from west to east in Western Africa.

Empires are formed when one becomes more powerful than another. The lesser empire is conquered, and its land, people, and customs are absorbed into the larger empire. In the case of Songhay, the original kingdom was Gao, a city on the Niger River, which was established as early as 680 CE. Its kings gradually increased their power until they began to rule over neighboring peoples. Together, all those peoples came to be known as the Songhay. In the 1590s, a civil war within the empire opened the door for Morocco, a powerful neighboring kingdom, to conquer the Songhay and end its reign as one of the great African empires.

CHAPTER ONE

The Peoples of Songhay

The Songhay Empire was the largest and the last of the three major precolonial empires to emerge in West Africa. It was composed of many different peoples—including the Sorko, the Gow, and the Do— who made their livelihoods from the Niger River and its bordering lands.

The Sorko were a tribe of fishermen who established settlements on the banks of the Niger River. They were considered masters of the water for their ability to build and operate boats and canoes on the river. Because the Niger was a strategic, agricultural, and economic lifeline for the Songhay Empire, the Sorko were dominated by the Songhay and were used for their boatbuilding and river navigation skills. The Gow people were hunters who specialized in killing river animals such as crocodiles and hippos. People known as the Do farmed the rich lands bordering the river. Prior to the tenth century, Songhay speakers joined these groups and took control over their ways of life and their lands. The area came to be known as Songhay.

The camel-riding Tuareg were among the earliest people of the region. They periodically rode out of the Sahara to the east to establish camps near the Niger River. They stored their trade goods in these camps and conducted business with others who used the river. Some of the Tuareg camps eventually grew into towns and cities. In about 679 CE, a Tuareg chief,

This brass anklet was worn by a member of the Sorko, a tribe of fishermen. The Sorko were adept at navigating the Niger River. They were dominated by the Songhay and became part of the Songhay Empire.

Za Alayaman, made his capital at Kukiya, which was downriver from Gao and near the present-day frontier between Mali and Niger. Alayaman founded the first known Songhay dynasty, or line of rulers. The rulers carried the title of *za*, which means "king" in the Tuareg language.

HISTORY ATTESTS TO SONGHAY'S ISLAMIC TRADITION

Songhay oral history—historical reports that are passed on from generation to generation by word of mouth—states that, in the year 1010, Za Kossoi officially converted to Islam. This improved relations with the Muslim traders, gave the za spiritual authority over his Muslim subjects, and increased his power.

Knowledge of Songhay history was greatly increased in the 1950s, when archaeologists made an important discovery in the village of Saney, near Gao. They found tombstones made of Spanish marble with Arabic inscriptions. These tombstones marked the graves of the kings of Gao, including Abu Abdallah Muhammad, who died in the year 1100. In Arabic, the name Abdallah means "slave of Allah" (God), signifying someone who is a devout Muslim. This discovery supports research that suggests that the kings of Gao were firmly entrenched in the Islamic faith and that their trade network extended all the way to Spain. The marble tombstones suggest that the kings were wealthy enough to import expensive goods from other countries.

The City of Gao

Between 750 and 950 CE, the city of Gao became an increasingly important trade center for goods being transported across the Sahara Desert. These goods included gold, salt, slaves, kola nuts, leather, dates, and ivory.

Some of the ivory was from elephant tusks. However, archaeologists (scientists who study the way humans lived a long time ago) have recently learned that the Songhay also exported hippo tusks from Gao. Furniture makers in North Africa and Spain preferred hippo ivory because it retained its

The city of Gao became a significant center for trade. Merchants traveled by camel from long distances to buy and sell their goods.

pure white color after it was cut into pieces. The pieces were then inlaid into beautifully carved wooden furniture.

The trade in such valuable products made the Songhay rulers wealthy due to the taxes they levied on all of the goods moving in and out of their territory. This rich trade grew, and Gao became the Songhay capital city.

Early West African traders did not use the kind of money that is in use today. Instead, they did business through a barter system, in which one type of product was traded for another. They did use small shells, called cowries, as currency. Their value was low. When the German traveler Heinrich Barth visited Timbuktu in 1853–54, he paid 13,500 shells for a single piece of cloth. Traders found these shells to be inconvenient to carry and use.

Many of the merchants involved in the trans-Saharan trade were Berber people, a group of Muslims who traded with the people living on the southern edge of the Sahara, including the Songhay. In both commercial and residential areas of Gao, mosques were established for the Muslim merchants. Later, as Islam became increasingly influential, the za of Gao allowed a mosque to be built in his part of the city.

The Birth of the Sunni Dynasty

Early in the 1300s, the Za dynasty of Gao was replaced by a new line of rulers, who carried the title of *sunni*, or *shi*, the meaning of which is uncertain. At this time, the Empire of Mali, which lay upriver from Songhay country, was the dominant force in the region of the upper Niger River.

Located in Timbuktu, the Great Mosque, also called the Djingereber, was constructed of dried mud bricks and stone rubble with clay rendering. Although this mosque and others in Timbuktu have been continuously restored, these historical monuments are being threatened by desertification.

For hundreds of years, the wealth and importance of Gao had been increasing because of its trade across the Sahara. Attracted by Gao's prosperity, the emperor of Mali, Mansa Musa, conquered the Kingdom of Gao in the early 1300s. This allowed Mali to control the Songhay people's trade routes and collect taxes from their rulers.

The second sunni of Gao, Sulayman Mar, later led the Songhay army against Mali. He regained Gao's independence from Mali around 1375. Under Sulayman Mar, Songhay remained only a small kingdom. His descendent, Sunni Ali, would turn the tiny kingdom into a mighty empire.

CHAPTER TWO

Empire Rising: Sunni Ali Takes Control

The greatest leaders of world governments and global corporations are often asked if it's better to be feared or loved. Is loyalty and unity best inspired by threats or by persuasion and accommodation?

The greatest hero of Songhay legend is Sunni Ali Ber, of the Sunni dynasty, and he clearly preferred to guarantee loyalty, obedience, and respect through threats of violence. Sunni Ali had no qualms about following through on those threats when provoked. He reigned from roughly 1464 to 1493. In the oral traditions recounted by Songhay storytellers, Sunni Ali is credited with building and expanding the Songhay Empire and was known as a formidable military strategist and conqueror. He was also known as a sorcerer who had magical power. Sunni Ali is still referred to in history as the "sorcerer king."

Guided by Spirits

Ali's mother was from a town called Fara, whose people were not strict Muslims. Their religious leaders were diviners and sorcerers who practiced the religion of their ancestors, which included worshipping spirits and showing respect for ancestors. These religious leaders were among the best-educated people in their society. They communicated with the spirit

This ancient copy of the Koran is housed in one of the libraries in Timbuktu. Many scholars believe there could be more than a million manuscripts in the city's twenty-two private libraries. Scholars also theorize that, before the European colonization, several million ancients texts and manuscripts were buried around the region to protect them from the wars that were waged over precious land and natural resources.

world to determine the causes of problems that arose in their community. Once they felt that the spirits had helped them identify the problems, traditional priests performed sacrifices in honor of the spirits. In this manner, priests were able to solve problems and cure diseases with the supposed help of supernatural guides and advisers.

This was the community in which Ali grew up, watched over by his mother and uncles. He was a Songhay prince and received some basic education in Islam. When he reached manhood, his beliefs were more in line with the ancient ways of magic and sorcery than with the Islamic faith. Later, when he came to the throne, he ruled over the Muslim traders and scholars who lived in the cities. Most of his subjects, however, were non-Muslim farmers, hunters, and fishermen of the countryside. Sunni Ali governed effectively by maintaining his association with both Islam and the religion of his ancestors.

A Changing of the Guard

The Songhay Empire emerged after a rebellion against the Mali Empire, which was then one of the largest empires in the world. The Mali Empire was located between the gold mines of West Africa and the Niger River floodplain, an agriculturally rich area. At its height, Mali comprised three states (Mali, Memo, and Wagadou) and twelve provinces that consisted of more than twenty million people living in more than four hundred cities, towns, and villages.

The Mali Empire broke down after political issues prevented a smooth succession of power. In addition, smaller cities within the empire began to want to break away and achieve independence in order to take advantage of the prosperous gold and salt trades. This led to rebellion in the city of Gao and the rise of the Songhay Empire, which took control of Mali's gold and copper mines, essentially ending Mali's rule.

Leading the rebellion was Sunni Ali, who is widely recognized as the first ruler of the Songhay Empire. Sunni Ali led the imperial expansion of the Songhay. Ali became sunni of Gao and the lands surrounding the city in about 1464. An ambitious ruler and military leader, Sunni Ali began his expansion of Gao by attacking the neighboring peoples who often raided areas that the Songhay regarded as their territory. Among those he attacked were the Mossi, the Fulani, and the Dogon. Once Sunni Ali had cleared Gao of its most immediate dangers, he turned his attention and his army to conquering Timbuktu, the second most important city in the region.

Timbuktu: A Cultural and Educational Center

Famous for its Islamic universities and the pivotal trading city of Jenne, Timbuktu was founded in about 1100 by the Tuareg

Timbuktu was a world center of Islamic learning from the thirteenth to the seventeenth century. Koranic schools, such as the one shown here, taught the Islamic faith, as well as the arts and sciences.

people. Populated mainly by Muslims, the city had a number of mosques where Muslims worshipped.

By the 1400s, Timbuktu had become an important gathering place. Located where the Niger River flows north into the Sahara Desert, this geographic position enabled the city to become a natural meeting point for the Songhay, Wangara, Fulani, Tuareg, and Arab peoples. Timbuktu grew into an important city. Its port was pivotal for trading goods (including gold, books, and salt) from West Africa and North Africa, and its multicultural society drew scholars and businessmen from African nations and the Middle East.

The city also became an educational destination for Muslim scholars of religion and for people looking to study other subjects. The city had a university, and a number of schools were built for the large number of scholars who came to Timbuktu in search of learning. The Muslim scholars of Timbuktu studied and wrote in the Arabic language. Devout in their Muslim faith, they believed that authority over people belonged not to rulers, such as Sunni Ali, but to Allah, which is the Arabic word for "God." The scholars defied Sunni Ali and refused to acknowledge his authority over them. As a result, Sunni Ali considered them enemies.

Harsh Punishment for an Insult

During this time period, Muhammad-n-Adda was governor of Timbuktu. He feared the growing power and approaching army of Sunni Ali. The governor was friendly and supportive of the powerful Muslim scholars and Tuareg leaders of Timbuktu, who were Sunni Ali's enemies. Hoping to escape punishment

This illustration of mid-nineteenth-century Mali shows the city of Timbuktu in the background. The city underwent numerous challenges, occupations, and wars. Today, modern-day Timbuktu is an impoverished city in the developing nation of Mali.

and to avoid a deadly siege of his city, however, Muhammad-n-Adda reached out to Sunni Ali. He sent him a letter saying that he would be happy to have Timbuktu become part of the Songhay Empire. Governor Muhammad-n-Adda died, however, before Sunni Ali and his troops ever reached Timbuktu.

Muhammad-n-Adda's son, Umar, became the next governor. Umar was not afraid of Sunni Ali as his father had been. Umar and the other leading men of Timbuktu did not believe that they should be subject to the authority of the Songhay kings. So Umar sent Sunni Ali an insulting message, bragging that he could fight off any attack by the Songhay armies.

In about 1469, Sunni Ali and his Songhay army arrived across the river from Timbuktu. Sunni Ali dominated the Niger River during his reign. He relied on a fleet of boats manned by Sorko crewmen under a naval commander, called the *hi-koi*. This navy fleet greatly strengthened the empire's military power and, with the command it exerted over the Niger River, provided the empire with significant control over trade routes.

The people of Timbuktu feared that Sunni Ali would inflict a terrible punishment upon them for defying his authority and cooperating with his enemies, the Tuareg. The Tuareg king supplied the frightened citizens with a caravan of one thousand camels, upon which they fled to Walata, a city in the Sahara Desert.

Meanwhile, Umar regretted the insulting letter he had sent Sunni Ali. In an attempt to make peace, he ordered boats to help Sunni Ali and the Songhay army cross the Niger River. Before the army entered Timbuktu, Umar escaped to Walata, leaving his brother al-Mukhtar to face the dreaded Songhay forces.

When Sunni Ali crossed the river and arrived in Timbuktu, he named al-Mukhtar the new governor. He ordered his troops to burn the city and kill anyone left behind as punishment for Timbuktu's defiance. Sunni Ali quickly earned the reputation of a repressive tyrant, known for destruction of cities and the torture and murder of enemy combatants and ordinary, civilian citizens of enemy states. Other accounts depict him as a masterful politician and military leader, one who brought great wealth and learning to his growing empire. What is beyond question is that Sunni Ali built and ruled the largest empire that ever existed in sub-Saharan Africa.

Conquering Jenne and Walata

The third most important city of the Songhay Empire was Jenne, far to the south of Timbuktu. Jenne had survived as an independent city due to being encircled by a high wall that protected it, its surrounding farms, and much of its cattle herds from invaders. The Niger River added to the city's security as well. During flood season, almost the entire city was surrounded by water.

Sunni Ali, intent on conquering Jenne, took advantage of the flood season by attacking the city with hundreds of warriors arriving on fleets of boats. The wall around the city proved to be too strong for Sunni Ali. So instead of scaling the wall for access to the city, he maintained a siege for seven years. Starvation eventually forced the people of Jenne to surrender.

Sunni Ali also wished to conquer Walata, located in the Sahara Desert. Walata grew in importance after the people of

ANGERING THE DEVOUT

Rather than follow the example of the Empire of Mali's style of rule, which included oppressive Islamic domination over non-Islamic people, Sunni Ali ruled his empire by mixing an observance of Islam with traditional African religion. This approach met with much disdain from Muslim clerics who lived in the cities, resulting in numerous attempts to overthrow Sunni Ali.

Timbuktu fled there when they were attacked by Sunni Ali in 1469. Sunni Ali was so attached to his fleet of boats that he even wanted to use them for a campaign against Walata, a desert city with no nearby water routes. In 1480, Sunni Ali had warriors dig a 120-mile (193-km) canal from Ras-el-Ma, at the western end of Lake Faguibine, through the desert to Walata. While his army was digging the canal, Sunni Ali learned that other invaders were attacking Walata. He quickly abandoned the canal project and marched his army over the desert to fight for control of Walata.

The Death of a King

In 1492, after holding power for twenty-eight years, Sunni Ali drowned while returning from battle. His son, Sunni Baru, succeeded him, but his reign was short, lasting only a year. Muhammad Toure, later called Askia the Great, staged a coup d'etat against Sunni Baru and established a new dynasty of Songhay rulers. Muhammad Toure and his descendants were strict Muslims. They reinstated orthodox observance of Islam and outlawed traditional African religions.

CHAPTER THREE

Askiya Muhammad: A Father and His Treacherous Sons

The greatest royal emperor in the history of the Songhay Empire was, in fact, neither royal nor one of the Songhay people. He was not part of the Songhay royal bloodline, had no inherent or hereditary right to be king, and possessed none of the sacred symbols that would allow him to assume power. Even more surprising, he was not an ethnic Songhay at all but was of Soninke lineage (the Soninke people founded the Empire of Ghana and eventually dispersed throughout Mali, Senegal, Mauritania, Gambia, and Guinea-Bissau).

This most unlikely of Songhay emperors was formerly one of Sunni Ali's army commanders. His name was Muhammad Abu Bakr Toure. The Toure were originally a clan of the Soninke people, whose connection with Islam dates back centuries. Muhammad Toure was a devout Muslim. Because of his faith, he objected to Sunni Ali's brutal treatment of the Muslims when he conquered Timbuktu.

In 1493, only fourteen months after Sunni Ali's death, Muhammad Toure and the troops loyal to him defeated the army of Sunni Baru, ending the Sunni dynasty. Muhammad Toure became the first *askiya*. Askiya was a rank in the Songhay

A member of the Tuareg tribe stands before a mosque in the Sahel region. The Tuareg are often referred to as "Blue Men of the desert" because their robes are dyed blue.

army. When Muhammad Toure became king, he took askiya as his title and as the name of his new dynasty. From that time on, all the kings of Songhay were known as askiya.

Building a New Power Structure

When Askiya Muhammad came to power, the Songhay Empire already had a well-developed system of government that had existed when Sunni Ali ruled, and perhaps dated to even earlier. The Songhay territory was divided into eleven provinces, each governed by an official with the title of *koi* or *fari*. These governors were usually relatives of the askiya. Important towns—such as Timbuktu, Jenne, Masina, and Tagha—had governors with the title of *munjo*. Their most important duty was probably to collect taxes.

Askiya Muhammad created a powerful new position in his government, called *kurmina-fari*. This official was the head of the western provinces of the empire. Other significant government officials were the *fari-munjo*, who were in charge of the royal lands; the *hou-kokorai-koi*, the master of the royal household; the *korei-farima*, who dealt with the neighboring Arab and Berber peoples; and the *wanei-farima*, who was responsible for the royal property acquired on military expeditions.

The chief military officers were the *hi-koi*, the master of the river fleet, and the *balama*, who was chief of Kabara, Timbuktu's port. *Qadis*, or senior judges, oversaw the legal system and were appointed by the askiya. The askiya himself also sat in judgment of legal disputes, as did the provincial governors.

Visiting Mecca

A significant teaching of Islam is the priority placed upon pilgrimage of all Muslims to Mecca. This is the birthplace of Muhammad the Prophet and the site of his first revelation of the Quran, or the main religious text of the Islamic faith. The Quran is believed to be the verbatim word of Allah. Mecca is located in present-day Saudi Arabia. This pilgrimage, or religious journey, is called the hajj.

Late in 1496, about three years after he came to power, Askiya Muhammad set off for Mecca. He was away for almost two years. The hajj added greatly to Askiya Muhammad's prestige. All who make the journey to Mecca acquire a special blessing called *baraka*, which is widely respected in the Western Sudan by Muslims and non-Muslims alike. Pilgrims also return with the special title *al-Hajj* (the Pilgrim). Furthermore, the sharif of Mecca—the spiritual leader of the Islamic world—named Askiya Muhammad as his caliph, or deputy, for the Western Sudan. This greatly increased Muhammad's power at home because it confirmed him as "Commander of the Faithful," or the leader of all the Muslims of the Western Sudan.

Askiya Muhammad, known as the "Pilgrim King," had the

Of the five pillars of Islam, the last is the hajj. It is stated in the Quran that every physically and financially able Muslim should make the hajj, or pilgrimage, at least once to the holy city of Mecca. The hajj takes place during the last month of the Islamic calendar.

wholehearted support of the influential Muslim population of the cities. This was in contrast to Sunni Ali, who made enemies of his primarily urban Muslim subjects while enjoying the loyalty of the Songhay who lived in the empire's rural communities. This was where the ancestral religion was still followed.

A Father Yields to His Sons

Authors of books written in Timbuktu state that Askiya Muhammad had thirty-four sons by his various wives and concubines. Since most of these children were half-brothers, related only through their father, they did not have the close attachment to one another that might be felt by brothers who all have the same mother. As Askiya Muhammad's sons grew up, they began to quarrel and compete among themselves for power. When Askiya Muhammad reached about seventy years of age, he began to weaken physically, and his sons began to demand that he retire in favor of one of them. He found it increasingly difficult to control his sons, some of whom were conspiring against him. The royal court became a dangerous place for the aging man.

One of his sons, Musa, who was considered a leader of the sons who demanded Askiya Muhammad's retirement, was appointed his father's heir. The younger generation of power-hungry sons were angered because Ali Fulan, a confidant of Askiya Muhammad who held the title hou-kokorai-koi, would not allow any of the sons to speak directly to their father. They did not know that Ali Fulan was concealing the fact that Askiya Muhammad had lost his eyesight. Musa threatened to kill Ali Fulan, who fled for his life in about 1527. In the following year, Musa led several of his brothers in a revolt against their father. In the process, they killed one of their own uncles, who had tried to calm them down.

In August 1528, during prayers at the mosque, Musa announced that his father had been removed from office. Old, blind, and without any powerful protectors, Askiya Muhammad had no choice but to abdicate. Musa became the next askiya of Songhay, although his father lived another ten years.

A Power Struggle Among Brothers

Askiya Musa had to fight his rival brothers to stay in power. He killed some of them in battle; others fled the empire. Those who remained in Gao began to disappear one after the other as Askiya Musa eliminated his rivals violently. Finally, in 1531, some of the surviving brothers joined together and killed Musa in battle. His bloody reign had lasted only two years and nine months.

The eldest of the remaining brothers was the kurmina-fari, or governor of the western provinces. He expected to be next in line for the kingship, so he returned to Gao. But when he and his supporting brothers arrived in the capital, they found that their cousin Muhammad Bunkan had seized the throne.

Askiya Muhammad Bunkan

Askiya Muhammad Bunkan is remembered for introducing music into his palace and for providing the members of his court with rich costumes of imported cloth. But Muhammad Bunkan led so many military campaigns and fought so many battles that the Songhay people grew tired of the constant conflict and the heavy toll of war. They began to dislike him. His popularity also diminished when people learned he was cruel to Askiya Muhammad the Great, who was now old and blind. Muhammad

This is the Tomb of the Askias at Gao, an unusual pyramid-style mud-brick structure built in 1495 by the first Askia emperor, Askia Mohamed, who was a great warrior. He is interred inside the tomb.

Bunkan forced Askiya Muhammad out of the palace and confined him to an insect-infested island in the Niger River.

Before long, Muhammad Bunkan made a mistake that would cost him his kingship. He brought back to Gao his childhood friend Ismail, one of Askiya Muhammad the Great's many sons. Ismail had been hiding with the Tuareg to escape the fighting between his brothers. Now he returned to Gao, where Askiya Muhammad Bunkan gave him one of his daughters as a wife. This was done on the condition that Ismail swear never to betray his old friend, who was now also his father-in-law.

Ismail was shocked to find that Muhammad Bunkan was mistreating his father, Askiya Muhammad, and humiliating his sisters by forcing them to appear at court with their faces uncovered. According to their Muslim beliefs, women who did not cover their faces were considered impure. When Ismail went to visit Askiya Muhammad on the island to which he had been exiled, the old king convinced him that Muhammad Bunkan had to be overthrown.

Askiya Muhammad's Sons Return to Power

Ismail worked with the many powerful friends of his father who were still in the court and deposed Muhammad Bunkan in April 1537. Muhammad Bunkan fled to Mali, and Ismail became the new askiya.

Askiya Ismail immediately released his father and brought him back to the palace. In gratitude to his son, Askiya Muhammad presented Ismail with his caliph's costume: a green robe, green cap, white turban, and the Arabian sword that Askiya Muhammad had been given in Mecca.

Askiya Muhammad the Great lived into his nineties and died in 1538, during Ismail's reign. Like Musa before him, Ismail reigned for two years nine months. But Ismail died of natural causes, in November 1539, rather than at the violent hands of his enemies. The peacefulness of his death was mirrored in the resulting succession of power. The leading men of Songhay agreed in a spirit of amicability and harmony to elect the next askiya. They chose Ishaq, another son of Askiya Muhammad.

Unfortunately, Ishaq was an ineffective and unpopular ruler because he upset many of the Songhay people. Although he was a devout Muslim, Ishaq regularly sent an agent to Timbuktu to demand large sums of money from the Muslim merchants there. This not only damaged the economy but also resulted in

Ishaq gaining many enemies. Frightened and suspicious that he would be overthrown, Ishaq killed or dismissed anyone he suspected of opposing him. He appointed three separate men as kurmina-fari. Ishaq executed the first one for an offense, and the second governor was caught in a conspiracy to overthrow Ishaq. The third kurmina-fari was Dawud, who eventually became the next askiya.

When Askiya Ishaq was near death, friends of Dawud called the governor of the western provinces to the capital to make sure he became the next askiya. They knew that Bokar, a handsome prince who was the son of one of Askiya Muhammad's daughters, was very popular with the people of Songhay. They feared he posed a threat to Dawud's bid to become king. Bokar did not survive this competition for power. According to legend, Dawud had him killed with a magic spell cast by a Muslim diviner.

The death of Askiya Muhammad the Great marked the beginning of the decline of the Songhay Empire. His sons and grandsons were mostly ineffectual rulers, and political intrigues and rivalries and numerous civil wars halted the empire's development and progress. Though Askiya Dawud provided a strong central authority that temporarily quelled the growing divisions in the empire, his death would renew the civil wars tearing Songhay apart from within. The result would be the once mighty empire's defeat and dismemberment at the hands of an emerging power—the neighboring state of Morocco.

CHAPTER FOUR

Dawud and the Beginning of the End

The reign of Askiya Dawud seemed to put the Songhay Empire back on track. Civil wars and internal strife ceased. His military campaigns led to territorial expansion. The empire seemed again to be growing, developing, and making its power and authority felt throughout sub-Saharan Africa. Indeed, together with Sunni Ali Ber and Askiya Muhammad the Great, Askiya Dawud is regarded as one of Songhay's three greatest rulers. His reign lasted for thirty-three years, from 1549 to 1582.

During the years of fighting between the rival sons of Askiya Muhammad, Songhay's enemies had begun to take advantage of the empire's internal conflict and seized on opportunities to raid its borders. Askiya Dawud moved to strengthen Songhay by leading successful military campaigns against old enemies. His only military defeat was in a raid far to the east against horsemen of the Hausa city-state of Katsina.

Promoting Peace, Consolidating Power

Askiya Dawud had received a solid Islamic education. He is said to have memorized the entire Muslim holy book, the Quran. Even after becoming askiya, Dawud continued his studies of

At Islamic schools, students learn to read and write Arabic. They also study the teaching of the Quran, which is the central religious text of Islam. Muslims believe the Quran is the verbatim word of God.

Islamic scripture and law. He was generous to Islamic scholars, giving them gifts of land, cattle, slaves, grain, and clothing. Timbuktu reached the peak of its prosperity during the reign of Askiya Dawud, and he contributed generously to the restoration of the main mosque there. When he passed that way on military campaigns, Dawud always stopped in Timbuktu.

Relations between the Songhay kings and the Timbuktu scholars had changed significantly since the days of Sunni Ali. The leading men of Timbuktu continued to believe that the Songhay kings had no real authority over them, a belief for which Sunni Ali had punished them so severely and violently when he had conquered the city in 1469. But Askiya Dawud, an educated Muslim himself, did not challenge the scholars' authority or independence.

Following Askiya Muhammad's abdication and up to the reign of Askiya Dawud, all of the rulers of Songhay had been Askiya Muhammad's sons, with the exception of the usurper Muhammad Bunkan. Many other sons of Askiya Muhammad had held high offices and titles throughout the empire. As these offices became vacant during the thirty-three years of Askiya Dawud's reign, he appointed his own sons to fill them.

Gradually, Dawud eliminated the descendants of his brothers, who were also sons of Askiya Muhammad, from high office. From then on, all the rulers of Songhay were descendants of Askiya Dawud. After Askiya Dawud died in 1582, however, warfare broke out once again throughout the Songhay Empire as his sons fought among themselves for power.

FAMILY LIFE

The Songhay society was patriarchal, or male-dominated. Men were allowed to have both wives and concubines (unmarried companions). This resulted in some men fathering hundreds of children, depending on the number of wives and concubines they had. When older brothers died, their goods and wives were passed down to younger brothers. When a father died, the eldest son became the leader of the family. But, as evidenced by the interfamily strife at the highest levels of Songhay society and rule, this system of succession did not always work smoothly or peacefully.

This is the inside of a tent house where families made their homes. Men and their wives or concubines lived in these structures with their children.

A Civil War Weakens the Empire

The next askiya was one of Dawud's sons, Askiya al-Hajj. Troubles between him and some of his brothers caused al-Hajj to be deposed in 1586. He was replaced by Muhammad Bani, another of Dawud's sons. Some of the Songhay people regarded Muhammad Bani as the most foolish of all the brothers. They tried to depose him, but their plot was discovered, and they were severely punished.

At the beginning of Muhammad Bani's reign, the town of Kabara was the scene of events that led to a civil war, which ultimately proved disastrous for the Songhay Empire. Kabara is Timbuktu's port, a few miles away on the Niger River.

At that time, two of the most powerful men in Songhay lived in Kabara. One of them was Chief Alu, the *balama*, or chief of the port, who was loyal to Askiya Muhammad Bani. The other was Muhammad Sadiq, the kurmina-fari, who was head of the western provinces and commanded the army of western Songhay. Muhammad Sadiq was also a son of Askiya Dawud and had good relations with the leading men of Timbuktu.

In 1588, Chief Alu beat and jailed one of Commander Muhammad Sadiq's men. In response, Sadiq killed Chief Alu. Since Alu was associated with Askiya Muhammad Bani, Commander Sadiq feared that the askiya, his brother, would seek revenge.

Sadiq and another brother, who was also an army commander, decided that their best hope was to combine their two armies, march against Gao, and attempt an overthrow of Askiya Muhammad Bani. This eventually led to a civil war, with

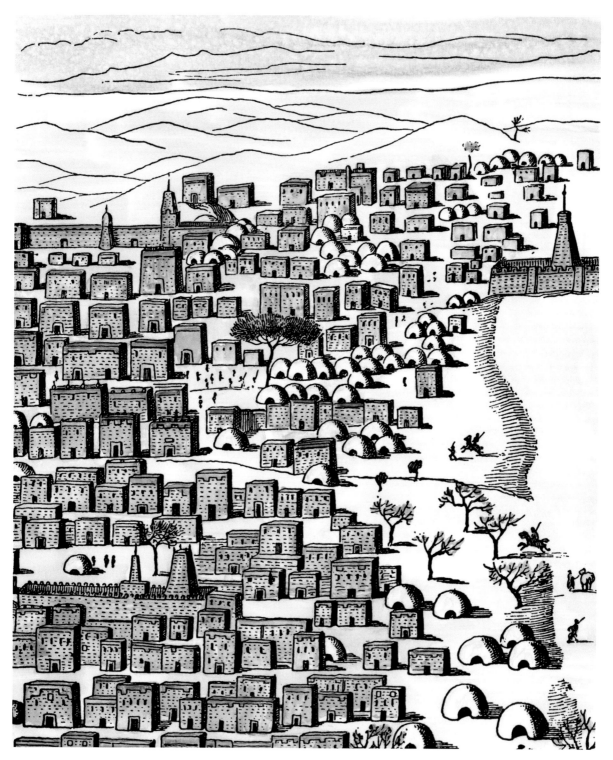

This 1828 drawing of Timbuktu by Caillie, the first European visitor to the city, illustrates how outsiders viewed the great African city.

the western Songhay army, led by Sadiq and based in Timbuktu, fighting the army of eastern Songhay, based in Gao and loyal to Askiya Muhammad Bani. The askiya died on the very day that the eastern Songhay army set out from Gao to meet Sadiq's western army.

After a bloody battle in which a great many troops were killed on both sides, the army of Gao defeated the troops from Timbuktu. Commander Muhammad Sadiq was hunted down and killed. All of the other army commanders of the western provinces, many of whom were princes of the royal family, were imprisoned.

The new askiya, Ishaq II, appointed new commanders, but he could not replace the troops that had been killed. Most of the soldiers who had supported Commander Sadiq never returned from battle. Songhay lost nearly half of its army as a result of this civil war. This weakened the empire to such an extent that it became vulnerable to attack from outside forces.

The most powerful of these outside forces were from Morocco and led by Sultan Ahmad I al-Mansur. His forces destroyed the salt mines that the Songhay economy depended upon. But the ultimate death knell was sounded by Morocco's superior military technology. Though greatly outnumbering the enemy invaders, the Songhay were no match for the Moroccans' gunpowder and firearms.

CHAPTER FIVE

An Empire Collapses, but a Legacy Endures

This illustration depicts slave traders returning to Timbuktu. Prisoners of war often became slaves and served their conquerors. When the Atlantic slave trade began, many began to be sold to European traders and were shipped to Europe or North America.

Relations between the Songhay Empire and Morocco were not always so fraught and contentious. In fact, they were long characterized by peacefulness, freedom of movement between states, two-way emigration, economic trade, and cultural exchange. For many centuries, Songhay had been involved in peaceful trans-Saharan trade with Morocco. Moroccan traders lived in Songhay, and Songhay merchants stayed in Moroccan cities.

The kings of Morocco were well informed about Songhay and were attracted by tales of its great wealth. For the weakened Songhay Empire, this presented a dangerous situation because Morocco was now at the peak of its power and eager to seize both territory and riches.

Vulnerability Empowers Morocco

Ten years before the Songhay civil war, in 1578, the Portuguese invaded Morocco with an army of twenty-five thousand soldiers. The Moroccans won a great victory over the Portuguese at the Battle of Al-Ksar al-Kabir. Only a few hundred Portuguese soldiers survived to tell the tale, while many others became prisoners of the Moroccans. This has been called one of the most decisive battles in world history. For many years, Portugal's defeat discouraged Europeans from attempting further efforts to conquer North Africa. It also showed how strong Morocco was at that time.

The sultan of Morocco, however, had been killed in his hour of victory. He was immediately succeeded by his twenty-nine-year-old brother, Mulay Ahmad, who received the title al-Mansur, meaning "the victorious." Sultan Mulay al-Mansur was a skillful ruler. He strengthened his kingdom through diplomacy and military campaigns that ended internal conflicts. His diplomats ensured good relations with foreign powers by offering rich gifts to their rulers. However, all of this gift-giving drained the Moroccan royal treasury.

Looking for a way to rebuild the Moroccan treasury, Mulay al-Mansur decided to capture Songhay's wealth. In 1583, five years before the Songhay civil war, he hired an Arab merchant named Ibn al-Filali, who lived in Gao. Al-Filali acted as a spy and reported back to Mulay al-Mansur with news about the Songhay Empire. When Mulay al-Mansur heard that a civil war had broken out between the western and eastern provinces of the Songhay Empire, he knew it was time to strike.

LE MARCHAND D'OR.

As a center of trade, Timbuktu hosted merchants who bought and sold goods. Here, as this illustration shows, a merchant and buyer settle on a price for goods.

The Conquest of Songhay

After the civil war broke out in Songhay, Ibn al-Filali informed Sultan Mulay al-Mansur that it had greatly weakened the Songhay Empire. In 1589, the Moroccans forged a letter that they claimed had been sent to the sultan by a brother of Askiya Ishaq II. The man they claimed was the askiya's brother was really a slave who had escaped from the Songhay royal household and fled to Morocco. In the forged letter, the askiya's "brother" asked Mulay al-Mansur to aid Songhay rebels in overthrowing the askiya.

The letter was sent to Askiya Ishaq II early in 1590, with a demand to surrender and accept Moroccan authority. Askiya Ishaq II failed to take this threat seriously. He was so unconcerned about the Moroccan forces that, instead of preparing for an invasion from the north, he took his troops on an expedition far to the west of the empire. Askiya Ishaq II and his troops were still far from home when they received news that the Moroccan army was on its way.

The Moroccan army had set out at the end of 1590 with 4,600 experienced fighters. They were led by Judar Pasha, a Spanish Christian who had converted to Islam. His army included many Portuguese and Spanish prisoners who had been captured by the Moroccans at the Battle of Al-Ksar al-Kabir twelve years earlier. Faced with imprisonment, slavery, or death, these prisoners of war chose instead to convert to Islam and serve in the Moroccan army. Among them were five hundred horsemen armed with guns, called arquebuses. These were the most modern weaponry of the day. An additional 1,500 horsemen carried long spears, and they took along ten cannons that fired stone cannonballs.

When the Songhay received warning of the Moroccan invasion, Muhammad Gao, who was then commander of the western troops, wanted his men to go out immediately and fill in the desert wells so that the invaders could not find water. This was a good plan, but the askiya ignored his advice. Instead, Askiya Ishaq II sent messengers to tribal chiefs asking them to fill in the desert water holes. The messengers never reached

THE RULING DYNASTIES OF THE SONGHAY

The earliest rulers of Gao went by the title of za. According to tradition, there were fifteen za up to the time of Za Kossoi, who converted to Islam in the year 1010. The Za dynasty continued for more than three hundred years until it ended in 1335 with the first of the kings known as sunni. During the time of the sunni, the Kingdom of Gao expanded to become the Songhay Empire. The sunni ruled until 1493, when Muhammad Toure founded the Askiya dynasty.

The three greatest kings of Songhay each led the empire through important periods of expansion. The first was from 1464 to 1492 under Sunni Ali. The second was from 1493 to 1528 under Askiya Muhammad the Great. The third was from 1549 to 1582 under Askiya Dawud. Historians believe there were twelve askiyas altogether, including Muhammad Gao and two others who bore the title after the Moroccan invasion:

Muhammad the Great	1493–1528
Musa	1528–1531
Muhammad Bunkan	1531–1537
Ismail	1537–1539
Ishaq I	1539–1549
Dawud	1549–1582
al-Hajj	1582–1586
Muhammad Bani	1586–1588

| Ishaq II | 1588–1591 |
| Muhammad Gao | 1591–1592 |

After Askiya Muhammad Gao was lured to his death by the Moroccan general Mansur, two other sons of Askiya Dawud held the title of askiya at the same time. One of them lived at Timbuktu as a puppet ruler of the Moroccan government. The other was at Dendi, where he continued to lead Songhay resistance against the Moroccan occupation.

their destinations. Instead, they were intercepted and attacked by Tuareg raiders.

If the Songhay had attacked while the Moroccans were exhausted from the two-month journey across the desert, they might have been victorious. But Askiya Ishaq II's troops had been quickly assembled and were disorganized. The Moroccans had a week to recover from their journey before the war began.

An Empire Ends

The decisive battle took place on March 12, 1591, at Tondibi on the east bank of the Niger River, about 35 miles (56 km) north of Gao. The Songhay army, with more than forty thousand men, could not compete with the superior firepower of Judar's disciplined and heavily armed troops. The Songhay suffered heavy losses. As they retreated across the Niger River, courageous Songhay soldiers tied themselves together and

This drawing shows a Tuareg warrior in his ceremonial dress. The Tuareg were renowned and respected fighters whose military might faltered only when firearms were introduced to West Africa and overwhelmed their skillful use of swords, lances, and shields.

continued to shoot arrows at the advancing Moroccans until the Songhay troops died in hand-to-hand combat.

Askiya Ishaq II offered the Moroccans a tribute of one hundred thousand pieces of gold and one thousand slaves, hoping this would pacify them and encourage them to leave the Songhay Empire alone. By that time, the Moroccan troops were exhausted and ill. Judar Pasha was prepared to accept the tribute and retreat back across the desert. However, Sultan Mulay al-Mansur wanted his army to occupy the newly conquered land below the desert. He angrily rejected Askiya Ishaq's offer and replaced Judar Pasha with another general, also named Mansur, who was instructed to complete the conquest of Songhay. The Moroccans occupied Timbuktu, Gao, and Jenne. They looted these cities and sent the wealth back to Marrakesh, where it was used to fill the treasury and build palaces.

The Songhay army had been defeated in battle and driven from the empire's trading cities. However, Songhay soldiers continued to resist the Moroccans with surprise attacks throughout the countryside. Succeeding askiyas continually sent raiding parties to attack Moroccan guard posts and troops. But the Songhay government had been weakened beyond recovery. The askiya's former subjects revolted, and Songhay kings were never able to recover their extensive powers or dominions. The Songhay Empire had fallen to the Moroccans.

The Songhay people, though vanquished and stripped of their empire, remained resilient. They went on to found the Dendi Kingdom, which held sway in what would become modern-day Niger, from 1591 to 1901. Its capital city was Lulami. After many futile decades spent trying to reestablish Songhay supremacy in West Africa, the Dendi Kingdom, weakened by a long string of unstable leaders, coups, and civil wars, succumbed to occupation by French colonial forces.

The Songhay Legacy

Together, the Songhay Empire and its predecessor, the Kingdom of Gao, formed a powerful West African state that lasted some nine hundred years, making it one of the longest to endure throughout global history.

The long reign of the Songhay can be credited to the empire's effort to bring contrasting cultures together, instead of repressing the traditions and beliefs of its newly conquered populations. Many other empires sought to force those they conquered to accept imperial religious beliefs, cultural traditions, and economic models, rather than accommodating and incorporating native practices. These empires may have had mighty and fearsome rulers. Without earning the loyalty and support of all of the people ruled in the dominion, however, many emperors throughout history found it difficult to maintain absolute rule over the lands they had conquered. As a result, their empires soon disintegrated and disappeared.

By contrast, the Songhay state developed a thriving trade network, a complex system of government, and a fairly tolerant and multicultural society. All of this made stability, prosperity, and expansion possible for many centuries.

CHAPTER SIX

The Songhay People Today

Today, the majority of the Songhay people (who number three to five million) live along the Niger River from Niamey, Niger, to Timbuktu, Mali. Modern-day Songhay are spread across a region that encompasses the Niger Bend area of Mali and portions of the Republic of Niger

The Songhay people remain skillful farmers, working the land around them. As seen here, many grind their own grain for food.

and northern Benin. Because of the many cultures that made up the Songhay Empire, this region is characterized by cultural influences drawn from a variety of ethnic groups. There are many languages and customs that are embraced by the people living in this area of Western Africa.

Modern-day Songhay people still speak native Songhay languages and refer to themselves by the name Songhay, which is now more of a historical rather than an ethnic designation. The majority of these people continue to follow Islam and Animism, which is the traditional belief that natural objects, natural phenomena, and the universe itself all possess souls. There continues to be a strong respect for the power of ancestors, and a reverent fear of the spirit world remains.

Through a combination of their strong Islamic and traditional tribal beliefs and ingrained cultural and social customs, the Songhay people have managed to resist the influence of Christianity and Christian missionaries who have attempted to convert them.

A Difficult Way of Life

Life for the Songhay people is not easy. Approximately 50 percent of the population is under the age of fifteen years old. The poverty level is so significant and medical attention is so lacking that three out of five Songhay children die before their fifth birthday.

Children are often not formally educated, and many will never learn to read. Once a child is old enough to walk and understand basic instructions, he or she begins to assist in family life. Children can often be found gathering firewood,

Today, the Songhay inhabit lands in what is now the country of Mali. The city of Gao is still operational, as is Timbuktu, which is also spelled "Tombouctou."

sweeping the family compound, or searching for food. Young girls often care for their younger brothers and sisters. Young boys join their fathers in preparing the fields for planting crops and grains.

It remains a patriarchal society in which men are in charge and property and title are inherited by male children. This has made life extremely challenging for women. Once girls become women, they usually enter into a continuous cycle of pregnancy and childbirth. Their religion dictates that men can take as many as four wives, and they often do so. This results in the even greater diminishment of status among women throughout society and even within the family unit.

FOODS

The Songhay maintain a diet of millet, which is a small-seeded grass. It is used to make *haini maasa* (pancake), *doonu* (porridge), or *howru* (paste). Millet paste, made by mixing millet flour with boiling water, is consumed at most evening meals. It is topped with a variety of sauces or peanuts. The Songhay make these sauces from common ingredients such as *tofunua* (ginger), *tonka* (hot pepper), and *gebu* (onion flour with sesame). Much of the diet is meatless, with few if any animals used in meal preparation.

Religious Life

Almost all Songhay are practicing Muslims. The Muslim religion requires that practitioners pray five times a day, avoid alcohol and pork, observe the one-month fast of Ramadan, and make an attempt to travel to Mecca at least once in their lives. As stated previously, the Muslim faith has not entirely banished traditional beliefs practiced since the height of the Songhay Empire. The Songhay regularly consult diviners (fortune tellers) and other traditional spiritual advisers, such as *sohancitarey* (sorcerers), *sorkotarey* (praise-singers to the spirits), and *zimatarey* (spirit-possession priests).

The Songhay celebrate both religious and secular holidays. The three major Muslim holidays are observed. These are Ramadan, which is the ninth month of the Islamic calendar and the month in which Muslims believe the Quran was revealed; Eid al-Fitr, which marks the end of Ramadan and is a day on which Muslims around the world show a common goal of unity; and Eid al-Adha, which honors the willingness of the prophet Abraham to sacrifice his young first-born son, Ishmael.

The Songhay celebrate the secular holidays of the particular countries in which they live—Mail, Niger, and Benin. These nonreligious holidays can vary based on local culture and customs.

Education and Work

There is both formal and informal education of Songhay children. Parents teach children common survival skills needed to

As did their ancestors, the Songhay still work the Niger River, building and navigating boats along its shores.

live successfully in society. These include farming, fishing, hunting, building huts and houses, cooking, weaving, and sewing. Many Songhay children attend elementary school, but illiteracy is common. Formal education is not valued since there is no industry and few jobs to which to aspire.

The main work is millet and rice farming and, on a seasonal basis, trading and tailoring. These require no formal education. Families find that educated children will leave the family to live in larger towns and cities, leaving them with no help on the farm or around the house. Life for the Songhay is extremely difficult and often characterized by unceasing labor, poverty, and illness. Yet they remain a proud and strong and enduring people, inspiring and worthy heirs to the empire that bears their name and furnishes their rich and influential legacy.

c. 679 CE The dynasty of rulers carrying the title of za is founded at Kukiya.

c. 750 Cao becomes an important trading city.

c. 1010 Za Kossoi becomes a Muslim.

c. 1100 Timbuktu is founded.

c. 1300 The Za dynasty of rulers is replaced by those carrying the title of sunni.

c. 1310–1330 Songhay begins to be ruled by Mali.

c. 1375–1400 Songhay regains its independence from Mali.

1464 Sunni Ali comes to power and begins to conquer neighboring peoples.

1468–1469 Sunni Ali captures Timbuktu.

1470–1476 Sunni Ali captures Jenne.

1492 Sunni Ali drowns while returning from a military campaign.

1493 Muhammad Toure ends the Sunni dynasty and becomes the first askiya.

1496–1498 Askiya Muhammad makes the pilgrimage to Mecca.

1528 Askiya Muhammad is removed from office and replaced by one of his sons.

1549–1582 Askiya Dawud reigns.

1591 Songhay is invaded by the Moroccan army and defeated at the Battle of Tondibi.

1660 The unified southern state of Songhay is broken into five principalities: Garuol, Tera, Dargol, Kokoro, and Anzuru.

1898 French colonial authority takes over rule of the five principalities.

1920 The first evangelical missionaries arrive in Timbuktu.

1988 Timbuktu added to UNESCO (United Nations Educational, Scientific, and Cultural Organization) World Heritage list.

2012 Gao and Timbuktu are captured from the Malian military by Tuareg rebels and Islamist militants.

2013 French and Malian troops retake Timbuktu from the Islamist rebels.

GLOSSARY

Allah Arabic word meaning "God."

animism The belief that natural objects, natural phenomena, and the universe itself all possess souls.

Arabic Language of Arabia; believed by Muslims to be the language in which Allah revealed the Quran to the prophet Muhammad.

archaeologist Scientist who recovers, studies, and interprets evidence about how people lived long ago.

arquebus Early type of firearm that employed a primitive method of igniting gunpowder.

askiya Title of a king of Songhay of the Askiya dynasty; originally a designation of rank in the Songhay army.

balama Chief of the port at Kabara, the port of Timbuktu.

baraka Blessing received by pilgrims who make the hajj.

depose To overthrow or remove from office.

diviner Priest or priestess who possesses special means of foretelling future events.

fari Government official; governor of a Songhay province.

fari-munjo Official in charge of the royal lands.

hajj Pilgrimage to Mecca and Medina undertaken by many Muslims in accordance with Muslim teaching.

Hajj, al- The Pilgrim; honorary title given to one who has made the hajj.

hi-koi Commander of the Songhay river fleet.

hou-kokorai-koi Official in charge of the royal household.

Islam Religion that holds that Allah is the one God whose teachings were transmitted directly to the prophet Muhammad.

koi Government official; governor of a Songhay province.

korei-farima Official responsible for Songhay relations with Arab and Berber traders and settlers.

kurmina-fari Governor of the western provinces and commander of its army, always of the royal family, second only to the askiya in power.

mosque Muslim house of worship.

munjo Governor of a major city.

Muslim Member of the Islamic faith.

precolonial Pertaining to the time before a region or country became a colony.

qadi Senior judge in Islamic society.

Quran The main religious text of the Islamic faith that was revealed to Muhammad by Allah; also known as the Koran.

secular Relating to worldly, rather than religious or spiritual, concerns; not overtly or specifically religious in nature.

siege Military blockade of a well-defended place to force it to surrender, often by creating scarcity of goods and starvation.

sorcerer Person with magical powers.

sultan Powerful, dominating Muslim leader.

usurper One who seizes power by force and without legal right.

wanei-farima Official responsible for the booty or spoils captured during military expeditions.

za "King" in the Tuareg language.

FOR MORE INFORMATION

African Cultural Center
P.O. Box 3147
Grand Central Station
New York, NY 10163
Web site: http://www.accenter.org
The African Cultural Center educates the general public
    about the diverse cultures in Africa through music,
    dance, the arts, and workshops.

African Cultural Exchange
120-35 142nd Street
Jamaica, NY 11436
(917) 862-2864
Web site: http://www.theafricanculturalexchange.org
This nonprofit organization is dedicated to providing cross-
    cultural links between North Americans and Africans.

African Studies Association
Rutgers University - Livingston Campus
54 Joyce Kilmer Avenue
Piscataway, NJ 08854-8045
(848) 445-8173
Web site: http://www.africanstudies.org
This organization was established in 1957 and is dedicated
    to sharing and disseminating information regarding the
    continent, kingdoms, and cultures of Africa.

African Studies Center
University of California, Los Angeles (UCLA)
10244 Bunche Hall
405 Hilgard Avenue

Los Angeles, CA 90095
(310) 825-3686
Web site: http://www.international.ucla.edu/africa
The African Studies Center at UCLA promotes the critical
and cultural study of the rapidly changing and complex
face of Africa in the twenty-first century.

African Studies/Columbia University Libraries
Lehman Library
420 West 118th Street
New York, NY 10027
Web site: http://library.columbia.edu/indiv/global/africa.html
Columbia University hosts one of the largest collections of
items related to African studies. The collection includes
information on the history, politics, and other subjects
related to African culture and history.

Association of African American Museums
P.O. Box 23698
Washington, DC 20026
(202) 218-7685
Web site: http://www.blackmuseums.org
The Association of African American Museums supports
African and African American focus museums nationally
and internationally, as well as the professionals who
protect, preserve, and interpret African and African
American art, history, and culture.

Michigan State University—African Studies Center
International Center
427 North Shaw Lane, Room 100

East Lansing, MI 48824
(517) 353-1700
Web site: http://africa.isp.msu.edu/about
Michigan State University (MSU) is a leading authority on
   African history and culture. More than 160 MSU faculty
   are working in thirty-two African nations—more than
   half the countries on the continent. Throughout the past
   decade, MSU has led the nation in the number of Africa-
   related doctoral dissertations produced. MSU also offers
   more than twenty-six study-abroad programs in Africa.

Museum for African Art
1280 Fifth Avenue, Suite 20A
New York, NY 10029
(212) 444-9795
Web site: http://www.africanart.org
The Museum for African Art is dedicated to increasing public understanding and appreciation of African art and
   culture. The museum is recognized worldwide as the
   preeminent organizer of exhibitions and publisher of
   books devoted exclusively to historical and contempo-
   rary African art.

Web Sites

Due to the changing nature of Internet links, Rosen Publishing
has developed an online list of Web sites related to the subject
of this book. This site is updated regularly. Please use this link
to access the list:

http://www.rosenlinks.com/EAC/Songh

FOR FURTHER READING

Armentrout, David. *Ghana, Mali, Songhay* (Timelines of Ancient Civilizations). Vero Beach, FL: Rourke Publishing, 2004.

Boye, Alida Jay, John O. Hunwick, and Joseph Hunwick. *The Hidden Treasures of Timbuktu: Rediscovering Africa's Literary Culture.* London, England: Thames & Hudson, 2008.

Brook, Larry. *Daily Life in Ancient and Modern Timbuktu* (Cities Through Time). Minneapolis, MN: Runestone Press, 2000.

Conrad, David C. *Empires of Medieval West Africa* (Great Empires of the Past). New York, NY: Chelsea House, 2009.

de Villiers, Marq, and Sheila Hirtle. *Timbuktu: The Sahara's Fabled City of Gold.* New York, NY: Bloomsbury Publishing, 2009.

Friedman, Mel. *Africa* (True Books). New York, NY: Children's Press, 2009.

Haywood, John. *West African Kingdoms* (Time Travel Guides). Mankato, MN: Heinemann-Raintree, 2008.

Jeppie, Shamil, and Souleymane Bachir Diagne. *The Meaning of Timbuktu.* Cape Town, South Africa: HSRC Press, 2008.

Marcovitz, Hal. *Islam in Africa* (Africa: Progress & Problems). Broomall, PA: Mason Crest Publishers, 2006.

McKissack, Patricia C., and Frederick McKissack. *The Royal Kingdoms of Ghana, Mali, and Songhay.* Clive, IA: Perfection Learning, 2010.

Mitchell, Peter, ed. *West Africa* (Peoples and Cultures of Africa). New York, NY: Chelsea House, 2006.

Nardo, Dan. *The European Colonization of Africa* (World History). Greensboro, NC: Morgan Reynolds Publishing, 2010.

Sheehan, Sean. *Ancient African Kingdoms* (Exploring the Ancient World). New York, NY: Gareth Stevens Publishing, 2010.

Shuter, Jane. *Ancient West African Kingdoms* (History Opens Windows). Mankato, MN: Heinemann-Raintree, 2008.

Wise, Christopher. *Timbuktu Chronicles 1493–1599, Ta'rikh al Fattash.* Trenton, NJ: Africa World Press, 2011.

Woods, Michael. *Seven Wonders of Ancient Africa.* Minneapolis, MN: Twenty-First Century Books, 2008.

INDEX

About the Author

Laura La Bella is a writer and editor. Among her books, she has written on subjects and issues relevant to Africa, including a profile of actress and activist Angelina Jolie in *Celebrity Activists: Angelina Jolie Goodwill Ambassador to the UN*; a report on the declining availability of the world's freshwater supply in *Not Enough to Drink: Pollution, Drought, and Tainted Water Supplies*; and an examination of the food industry in *Safety and the Food Supply*. La Bella lives in Rochester, NY, with her husband and son.

Photo Credits

Cover, p. 28 Nigel Pavitt/AWL Images/Getty Images; cover (background), p. 1 Triff/Shutterstock.com; p. 4 Eric Fefersberg/AFP/Getty Images; pp. 7, 11, 34, Werner Forman/Universal Images Group/Getty Images; p. 9 Tony Wheeler/ Lonely Planet Images/Getty Images; p. 14 Luis Davilla/age fotostock/SuperStock; p. 16 John Warburton Lee/SuperStock; p. 18 Universal Images Group/Getty Images; pp. 23, 47, 51 Frans Lemmens/Lonely Planet Images/Getty Images; p. 25 Fayez NureldineAFP/Getty Images; p. 32 Marka/SuperStock; p. 36 © North Wind Picture Archives; p. 38 Iberfoto/SuperStock; p. 40 Fotosearch/Archive Photos/Getty Images; p. 44 DEA/G. Dagli Orti/De Agosini/Getty Images; p. 49 © iStockphoto.com/chrispecoratro; back cover daulon/Shutterstock.com; cover, back cover, and interior pages graphic elements R-studio/Shutterstock.com (gold texture), brem stocker/Shutterstock.com (compass icon), Konyayeva/Shutterstock.com (banner pattern.)

Designer: Michael Moy; Photo Researcher: Marty Levick